GHOS
GHO
SHRE JBURY

Ghostly Goings-on in a Medieval Town

GHOSTS & GHOULS *of* SHREWSBURY

Ghostly Goings-on in a Medieval Town

JAMES I. PATTERSON

HALSGROVE

First published in Great Britain in 2009

Copyright © 2009 James I. Patterson

British Library Cataloguing-in-Publication Data
A CIP record for this title is available from the British Library

ISBN 978 1 84114 931 8

HALSGROVE
Halsgrove House,
Ryelands Industrial Estate,
Bagley Road, Wellington, Somerset TA21 9PZ
Tel: 01823 653777   Fax: 01823 216796
email: sales@halsgrove.com

Part of the Halsgrove group of companies
Information on all Halsgrove titles is available at: www.halsgrove.com

Printed and bound by Short Run Press, Exeter

CONTENTS

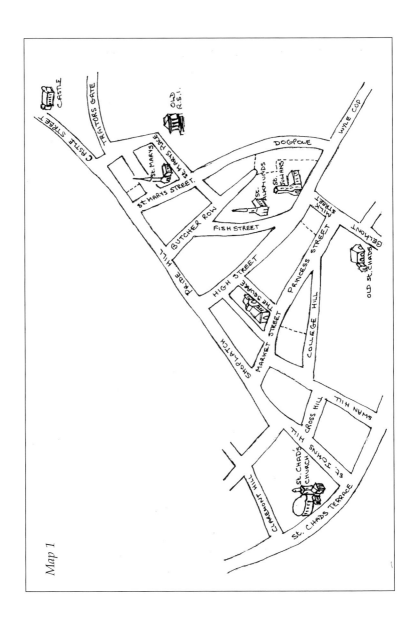

Map 1

6

Map 2

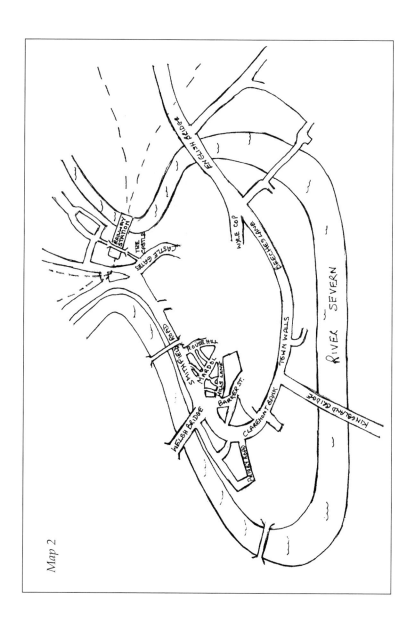

ACKNOWLEDGEMENTS

The author wishes to thank all of those who supplied or allowed photography and especially his wife Patsy Patterson for all her photographic work and support, and Pete Jones at the Clip Joint.

BY WAY OF AN INTRODUCTION

SHREWSBURY, or Scrobbs-by-rig as the Saxon founders of the town knew it, sits high on a rocky pinnacle almost surrounded by the mighty River Severn as it makes its way from the mountains of Snowdonia to the sea.

The people of this Welsh Marches town grew rich on the trade in wool and leather during the time that the river was navigable all the way down to Bristol and beyond. Woollen cloth was loaded onto barges at the foot of the Devil's Boundary westward bound for the Americas to clothe their slaves or eastwards to put clothes on the backs of Russia's peasants.

As a busy trading port with a perfect defensive position on the turbulent Welsh borders, Shrewsbury was once the third most important township in the country after York and London. It drew people to it from all over the British Isles and as far away as Germany and the Low Countries. Not all came as law-abiding traders – and not all passed over into the next life when death came a-calling.

The town has over 600 ghosts many of which have been confirmed by paranormal researchers. The ghosts still walk the streets and narrow passages [or 'shuts' as they are called locally] which have remained virtually unchanged since the thirteenth century. Walking through this, England's best preserved medieval town on a dark winter's night, it is all too easy to feel as though you are not alone. And sometimes, just sometimes, you <u>know</u> you are not alone. Sudden temperature drops; orbs of light, smells of lavender or smoke; maybe even the lightest of touches that will brush your shoulders or hair. The certainty is so overpowering that there is no need to see a physical reality, although ghosts and wraiths do show themselves from time to time especially [as folklore would have it] to those people born at midnight.

But why has Shrewsbury more ghosts than any other town in England? The answer is again found in ancient folklore. It tells us that any soul which can't leave this world for the next can only find peace by water – and the encircling waters of the Severn welcome them all, the good and the bad, with open arms.

I regularly lead ghost walks through Shrewsbury and this book is by way of being a guide to the town through its ghosts and ghouls. Come with me then and let me introduce you to just some of our forebears … If you dare!

THE GHOSTS
OF THE
STONE BRIDGE WARD

THE ENGLISH BRIDGE

There has certainly been a bridge standing on the road east out of Shrewsbury for over one thousand years. In the years immediately following the Norman invasion of England they linked the town to their Abbey of St Peter and St Paul by means of a nine hundred feet long wooden structure which spanned the whole flood plain. Eventually their bridge was replaced by one built in stone, hence the Stone Bridge and as it carried the road eastwards into England, it took on its more popular name of the English Bridge. Today it still hurries traders and townsfolk about their business, only those visitors on a pilgrimage to the Norman Abbey are fewer in number.

It should come as no surprise then that the ghostly figure of a Benedictine monk from the Abbey, huddled into his dark robes as if trying to afford himself some relief from the ever-present chill wind, is often reported hurrying across the river.

On the town side of the bridge lies an area of modern apartments and eighteenth century run-down shops. Once known as Bulgerlode, it was the place where leather bags were once fashioned. These shops together with an old foundry which is tucked away out of sight and famous for making the chains which still support the Menai Bridge at Anglesey stand on very old foundations. And it is here in two of these basements that we have some very strange, ghostly phenomena.

Firstly there are the light orbs. Walk into the pitch blackness of the cellars where you literally can't see the hand in front of your face, wait quietly for a moment and then take a photograph.

The result is … Nothing! Blackness stares back at you.

However, instead of waiting quietly try yelling or making a loud, sudden noise whilst at the same time pressing the shutter of the camera. The cellars fill with light orbs or energy

Outline of a ghost horse.

Light orbs.

fields which move this way and that. They are never the same in number or configuration.

I do not profess to understand it but these orbs of light do seem to be a very common occurrence in Shrewsbury taking place in many different premises and locations within the town. As such we will undoubtedly have to return to the topic later.

Then of course the photographs reveal some strange results. Look carefully at the photograph on page 12. Close scrutiny will reveal a ghost horse. The front legs are the clearest feature yet the horse's head is looking at you almost quizzically.

The horse is believed to have belonged to a cavalier from the time of the Civil War. In the August of 1642, Charles I arrived in Shrewsbury at the head of a seven thousand strong force of men-at-arms. When he moved on after about three weeks he left his relative, Prince Rupert, in charge of the royalist garrison. Amongst those soldiers was a mounted Dutch cavalier, who was billeted in the Dun Cow public house close to the Abbey on the Foregate.

The public house is inhabited by a monk with a sense of humour as he moves things around from room to room. He has been joined by our Dutchman who has not been able to leave this world for the next either. It seems that not long after his arrival he was upset by a servant in the Dun Cow and so ordered his hanging.

Prince Rupert was not pleased. He was already unpopular with the local inhabitants as he had allowed his army to eat them *'out of house and horse'* as well as making them work on the defences of the town. He needed the townspeople's cooperation and maybe that is the reason why he ordered the Dutchman's execution.

On the gallows the condemned royalist was still somewhat perplexed saying, *'But I only killed one Englishman.'*

One was enough. The execution went ahead. He has been seen in full cavalier garb both in the toilets of the Dun Cow as well as walking through the occasional wall or two. One man on holiday from Scotland was so affected by spotting the ghost that he ran from the premises spilling his drink on the way and later phoned the landlord asking him to send his luggage on. He was not going back!

But what of the horse in the photograph still inhabiting the cellar down on Bulgerlode some three hundred yards away?

14

A cavalier on horseback has been seen on the road outside the cellar-come-stable and also further up the hill into the town centre near the Nag's Head public house. More on that public house later, but I feel there is enough of a coincidence to say that our executed Dutchman is still riding from the Foregate to Prince Rupert's military headquarters in the centre of town. Maybe he liked the stabling arrangements on Bulger-lode where his horse would be safer on the other side of the guarded bridge. Whatever the truth of the matter the cavalier and his horse are still with us today.

THE UNICORN

At the end of the natural flood plain at the foot of the Wyle Cop and no more than fifty yards from our previous location stands the old black and white building which was formerly known as the Unicorn Hotel. It was one of the town's premier coaching inns during the eighteenth and nineteenth centuries.

The building may now have been sub-divided into a wine merchants, restaurant, professional treatment rooms and apartments, but the previous occupants haven't moved out.

There are a number of ghosts present but probably the most famous is the black cat. Just about everyone who has visited the premises has seen this apparition although first thing in the morning is the best time to catch a glimpse of it. The cat seems to be startled by the door opening and so runs from somewhere behind it, crosses the room in full view of the person entering and then disappears through a locked door.

Part of the Unicorn.

An old pendulum clock which is kept on the ground floor had its chiming mechanism dismantled over a quarter of a century ago. There is nothing to make it work any more and it didn't – until it came to be placed in the Unicorn Hotel. Now it chimes away merrily, mechanism or not.

Doors open and close, things are moved around and it is all very strange. When a psychic researcher visited it came as no surprise when he found three *'presences'* in the old building with *'an atmosphere'* in several rooms.

One of these presences is believed to be that of a travelling man called John Ludlow who carried all his cash around with him wherever he went. Now John Ludlow really enjoyed coming to Shrewsbury and staying in the Unicorn in particular and as a regular visitor he was always allocated the same room.

In 1840 he visited once more but unfortunately for him he was being followed. A young, petty criminal from Birmingham called Josiah Misters was intending to kill Ludlow whilst he slept and rob him of his fortune.

A sixth sense warned Ludlow that something was not quite right and so he moved bedrooms at the last moment. Josiah, waiting hidden in the room was thwarted but undeterred and when his intended victim moved on the following morning he followed.

The next night John again moved rooms at the last moment but unfortunately the hotel owner hired out the room to someone else. When the man went to sleep Josiah came out from under the bed and slashed his victim's throat with a cut-throat razor.

John Ludlow had been very lucky so he was able to return again and again to take his pleasures at the Unicorn, no doubt thankful for his life being spared. It is no wonder the psychic researcher said of the *'presences'* that they were happy and harmless.

HWYLFA COPPA

From the Unicorn the road into town now begins the steep climb up Hwylfa Coppa meaning *'the road up the hill to the top.'* Today it is better known as the Wyle Cop. It is fair to say that historically this part of Shrewsbury has probably been the most violent in the past. One of the three most lawless suburbs of yesteryear, Coleham, lies just beyond the river and in the time of the 'Navvies' – the gangs of men who arrived in the town to construct the canals and railways during the 1800s – the Cop became a 'no-go' area for any decent citizen. It is also the most evil part of Shrewsbury. There are things here which even our psychic investigators shy away from. We'll start with the worst of all, the Nags Head public house.

THE NAG'S HEAD public house or to give it the full title, the Nag's Head Without [as in 'without' being outside the town walls] dates from the 1300s.

From the roadway outside the top window is easily seen. In that room there is a cupboard which has a crude painting of an Old Testament prophet or the devil on the inside of its doors. Even modern-day paints are incapable of obliterating the figure which just comes back through the new coatings within days.

There have been three deaths in that room over the years which have but one connection. All the deceased were happy.

The first involved a man who had just been promoted to the position of coachman. He was staying in that room on the night before his first trip to London in charge of a coach and six. He hung himself.

The second case involved a young woman who was staying the night and due to leave on the first coach next morning with her young man. They had tickets to take ship to the New World and a new life together. She threw herself out of the window and died on the street below.

Prophet or devil?

The last death was that of a soldier returning from the nightmare of four years in the trenches of the First World War. On his first night back home and he shot himself.

That evil painting has been blamed for the horrors which happened in that upper room.

In more modern times the licensee of the public house was sleeping on the premises when he was woken by the sound of music coming from his juke box which he kept in the bar. It was 3 a.m. and positive that he was being burgled he armed himself with a billiard cue before creeping up to the door. He paused to listen. The music was still blaring so he threw the door open to confront the intruder, only the bar was in darkness – and silent. On checking the juke box he found that it was not even plugged in to the electric socket.

Recently a town guide visited the premises and was allowed to view the painting. She fell on the steep stairs on the way out. That may have been an accident, but shortly after that my wife and I visited to photograph the painting for this book and within two minutes of leaving the public house we were nearly killed by a 'run-a-way' car. Is that coincidence or enemy action?

A pause for breath at this point as I should have given you some tips earlier on how to protect yourself from evil. It may be a bit late for the Nag's Head but there is more to come so you may need this advice gleaned from years of research into 'the old ways.' First of all a protective amulet which is easy to carry is a simple sea shell. I've no idea why, it is just a piece of knowledge passed on from previous generations. The second means of protection needs no physical item about your person. Place your thumb between the forefinger and the middle finger then make a fist. Say the words, *'Four fingers and a thumb witch, I defy thee,'* and the evil spirit will avoid you. Lastly, spitting is good especially as you cross water. Spit three times into the water below as you cross to ensure a safe passage from the spirits who inhabit their watery world and who would just love to drag you down there to be with them. These water spirits are fine with humans provided you don't enter the water. If you do they can become very nasty indeed.

BARRACKS PASSAGE

Opposite the Nag's Head public house on the Wyle Cop is a line of original buildings all of which date from the early 1400s. Those timber framed dwellings and shops contain

Barracks Passage.

narrow passages or 'shuts' between and behind them and it is to one of the larger alleys, Barracks Passage that we now turn our attention.

This is a worrisome place, but first an example of nice, passive ghosts. Just before the Battle of Bosworth Field in the

August of 1485, Henry Tudor [who was to become King Henry VII] lodged in the building which fronts onto the incline of the Cop. The building also goes across the top of the 'shut' by which people enter Barracks Passage and the Lion Tap public house. That public house was where Henry Tudor's bodyguard, French and Welsh soldiers, were billeted during their stay. Because of the way in which the battle was fought, this bodyguard found themselves in the thick of the fighting almost immediately and they took an awful lot of casualties. The spirits of the dead soldiers returned to the Lion Tap, no doubt because they had such a good time in the town before their death. Even today groups of soldiery dressed in the garb of their time can be seen moving about inside the premises with one pressed into the shadows outside as though standing guard. At times their faces are pressed up against the windows.

Above the alley's overhang are a couple of small windows. The face of a female ghost appears looking down into the 'shut.' Her reasons remain unknown but she does no harm to anyone. The same cannot be said of our next visitor from the spirit world.

Imagine it is a snowy day in mid-winter and that there is a light covering of virgin snow on the cobbles of Barracks Passage. A young police constable ambles under the overhang and disturbs a hawk feasting on a small bird. Once disturbed it flies off leaving a small speck of bright red blood on the snow. That young constable was me and as I found this event extremely unusual [you do not see much wildlife in a Yorkshire mill town] I headed off to find the senior constable of the shift who knew everything there was to know about Shrewsbury.

'Get back down there quick,' I was told. *'You might see something you'll never forget.'* Well, the old constable was quite right. I still get goose-bumps thinking about it now nearly forty years later.

Just at the spot where I'd left the spots of blood there was a shape. It was about four feet high and completely covered from head-to-toe in a rough woollen cowl of the type used by monks. Only this cowl had no holes for the eyes or arms and no feet protruded from the bottom. I got the impression it may have been female but there were no identifying features except to say that this creature exuded absolute evil. There is no other way to describe it. It exuded absolute evil.

It made off down the alley and I made off in the opposite direction. *'Did you see anything?'* asked the old constable a few minutes later.

'No,' I lied hoping that my ashen face would not give me away. I may have been young but I was not stupid. To speak of what I had witnessed would have branded me as a complete – well – I would never have lived it down in the eyes of my colleagues.

'That's a shame,' replied the constable. *'I've heard of the hawk only once before and this old tale is maybe a hundred or more years old. On that occasion, just at the place you described, a woman's horse bolted for no reason and she nearly died from the fall.'*

I now believe that the creature I saw was something called a 'wraith.' It comes to warn of death or at least something bad that is about to happen. For me it was the death of a family pet the very next day but this creature is not something I would like anyone to ever encounter.

THE LION HOTEL

The Lion Hotel stands proudly at the top of the Wyle Cop with its front door guarded by a magnificent golden lion. The hotel was given a face-lift in 1777 disguising the fact that it is really three original early fifteenth century houses. There are a number of ghosts associated with this ancient coaching inn which has attracted the rich and famous throughout its history. Royalty, politicians, musicians, writers such as Dickens, all have walked through its rooms and no doubt marvelled at the world-famous Adam Ballroom on the first floor.

And we have one known ghost associated with the ballroom – The Grey Lady. She is regularly seen and variously described as *'an old lady dressed in powder grey'* and *'tranquil.'* Those descriptions did not stop one night porter handing in his notice.

The Grey Lady is seen standing at the foot of the staircase which leads to the ballroom. She is not the most attractive of women so that probably explains why it took a long time for her to find herself a young man. He was to meet her at the foot of the staircase and escort her to a dance being held in the Adam Ballroom and there announce their intention to marry to anyone who was anyone in Shrewsbury. A true commitment and once made, a commitment very hard to get out of.

Her beau never turned up and she is still waiting. She exits the building through a wall which used to be a door-

The Adam Ballroom.

way to the outside at one time and disappears half way across the alley as if she is mounting the steps of a waiting carriage.

The Grey Lady is also seen looking down onto the dance floor from the musicians' gallery and in a first floor corridor now only used by the staff of the hotel.

The ballroom is also the place I first became aware of the energy or light orbs which can fill this unique room. In my capacity as a town guide I was taking a tour one evening and recounted the sad tale of the Grey Lady when someone took a photograph on a digital camera. And there was an orb of light. The normal explanations and rationalizations were trotted out. They were specks of dust or a trick of the light and then a husband and wife stepped forward. Both took simultaneous photographs with their similar cameras. One of them captured – nothing, just total darkness even though the lights of the chandeliers were on. The other had hundreds of orbs filling the room. It was as if the dancers of times gone by had left their energy and vibrancy behind.

We have been lucky enough to visit an old gaol in Hobart in Tasmania to take a ghost tour. It was quite atmospheric and enjoyable but when we got to the execution chambers [one above the other for obvious reasons] my pen refused to work. It was fine everywhere else, but not there. Our guide expressed no surprise as he was used to any form of equipment refusing to work in the death chambers although it was usually cameras not pens.

I cannot help but think of that husband and wife team and the hundreds of orbs of light every time I enter the Lion.

Before we leave this lovely old hotel we must return to our cavalier from about 1642. It was Easter, 2007. A couple from Yorkshire awoke in Room 215 to find a cavalier in the full dress uniform of the Civil War period standing at the foot of their bed.

It came as a shock to them as this was a previously un-reported ghost. It begs the question as to whether it could be the same royalist soldier that we've met already.

ST JULIANA'S SHUT

St Juliana's, or St Julian's, Shut lies at the side of the Saxon church dedicated to St Juliana, a fourth century female martyr who carried out a long verbal contest with the devil. The 'shut' stands at the top of a flight of stone stairs leading from the flat piece of ground found at the top of the Wyle Cop. Today that short roadway is officially an extension of the Cop, but I prefer its medieval name of Baker Row. [Just as an aside I feel as though we, as the people of a town, lose a lot of our history by unnecessary changes to the names of ancient streets.]

St Juliana's Shut will be forever connected to the name of the Lion Hotel by the ghost found here.

During the nineteenth century a guest broke his stagecoach journey in Shrewsbury and stayed at the Lion Hotel. After din-ner he decided to go and have a brief walk around the town before turning in for the night during the course of which he visited St Juliana's churchyard no doubt attracted by the two different colours of stone from which the tower is made.

He turned in for the night and at 3 a.m. an upstairs maid was sent to rouse him from his slumbers. The stagecoach departed for London at 5 a.m. and on the first ring of the bells the coach was up and away. The early knock would allow the travellers time to breakfast, have a wash, re-pack and use the toilet.

The only thing was the maid found the man dead in his bed and so called the manager. He confirmed the death and so made a search of his belongings. Unfortunately there was nothing to identify the man who'd been travelling from Dublin to the capital city but he did have some cash. The manager called the undertaker and paid for a quick burial out of the man's own money. At 5 a.m. the stranger was being buried in the churchyard of St Juliana's instead of being on the coach for London. I cannot help but think of how tenuous our hold on life is as I don't suppose for one moment the man considered he was to spend the rest of eternity in the churchyard he liked in Shrewsbury.

Shortly after the undertaker had left strange noises began to be heard coming from the graveyard. They were described as *'wailings'* and *'scratching noises'* which were heard by the Tarbuck family who lived close-by. They were so frightened that they locked their doors and windows and retreated to the far side of their house until the noises stopped.

The next day they informed the town authorities of what they had heard and the undertaker was ordered to exhume the body of the stranger who'd recently died in the Lion. This he did and found that the man was indeed dead. Only now the flesh from his fingers and thumbs had gone, worn down to the bone by his frantic efforts to get out of the coffin. He'd been buried alive. This may not have been such an unusual occurrence as sometimes people were buried with a rope or some such tied to their toe which was then attached to a bell outside the grave. In that way if they'd been buried mistakenly then someone could effect a rescue – hopefully before the air ran out.

This story was told by a town guide to a group of men-folk who all burst out laughing. They were all Canadian undertakers and supplied the moral of this sad tale: *'Always buy a cheap coffin – they are easier to get out of.'*

As for the stranger no one knows to this day who he was or where he was from, but on a windy, dark night listen closely and you can still hear his wailing calls and the scratching noises as he fights for his life six feet underground.

MILK STREET

Directly opposite the main entrance to St Juliana's Church is Milk Street which was the centre of the dairy industry in Shrewsbury during medieval times. There are four premises in this street which is no more than fifty paces long which are haunted but we'll begin with the one building which is directly associated with the Davies family who were dairy workers and who lived and worked at number 4A.

4A MILK STREET

This small shop now sells children's clothes but back in the 1500s it was occupied by a Mr and Mrs Davies who worked turning milk into butter and cheese. They had two sons, Bryn and Daniel, who were abducted then kept in a locked room nearby and starved to death.

The offender and reason for this is lost in time but I have a theory involving an evil spirit called 'Bad Tom' who resides in the tiny street. But I will return to him later.

This is the only premises in Shrewsbury which has a full family of ghosts present. The boys could not pass on to the next world without their parents and the parents had no wish to leave without their children. Now they are re-united in their old home.

THE OLD POST OFFICE

A few yards away from the Davies family we find the fifteenth century coaching inn called The Old Post Office which is tucked away behind the medieval street and protected by the ancient buildings which crowd in upon its tiny courtyard.

To give some context as to just how old the buildings are, at school we learned a little ditty:

'In 1492 Christopher Columbus sailed the ocean blue.'

When Columbus sailed away and discovered America, these buildings were over fifty years old.

This coaching inn has several ghosts of its own, some of which have been confirmed by the psychic researchers.

The name 'Post Office' does not refer to the post as we know it today. Like the other premises we have already visited, The Old Post Office was a coach stop on the road from London to Dublin, the post being the stagecoach on which people travelled the length and breadth of the country. As a coaching inn catering for such passengers, the immediate area was full of overnight stabling for the horses. In fact at the peak of stagecoach travel there were hundreds of horses in Shrewsbury every night. Some estimates put it as high as six hundred.

And horses need caring for. There is still the ghost of a blacksmith working away at his forge and anvil beating out replacement horse shoes, repairing tack and making metal rims for the stagecoach wheels. He remains invisible toward the back of the courtyard, but the unmistakable sounds of a smithy at work are clearly heard on occasions.

The small courtyard also boasts the ghost of a Lavender Lady or Lavender Sally. The horses created an awful lot of manure and so the area smelled quite badly. To combat the foul odours gentlefolk would buy nosegays, small posies of lavender and other sweet smelling plants and flowers, which they would hold beneath their noses. One such lavender seller is still here and announces her presence by filling the courtyard with the unmistakeable smell of her wares.

Beneath the courtyard are the cellars. The trapdoor for the draymen to deliver the barrels of beer is still easily spotted by the wall of the public house. It is as close as we can get to our third ghost, a murdered girl who used to be a servant in the public house. She has been identified as 'Elspeth' who was raped and strangled with her body being left in the cellar for a while until the coast was clear. The murderer then returned to carry the unfortunate Elspeth to the River Severn before dumping her lifeless body into it. No doubt he was counting on the constant and savage undercurrents to drag her body down and take the evidence away.

Although her body was retrieved the murderer was never found. Could there be yet another connection with Bad Tom? Was he responsible for the deaths of the two Davies brothers and Elspeth? Both cases were in the late 1500s but we will return to that connection momentarily.

First we must enter the Old Post Office and bring things into the twenty-first century.

Only a few years ago a trainee manager of a local super-market lodged in Room 5. He was a typical young man being untidy and quite content to leave his room strewn with his discarded clothes. He would fall asleep with maybe the tele-vision or radio on and maybe a half-finished drink by his bedside.

Each morning he'd wake up to find that he had been properly tucked in and the room tidied to the point of per-fection. Even the Gideon Bible was carefully arranged on his bedside table. He was too embarrassed to say anything at first and became far too ashamed to mention it as this went on night after night. The time came for him to leave and as he shook hands with the landlady he plucked up enough courage to thank her for tucking him in every night and tidying up after him. The reply sent a chill down his spine. *'I have never been in your room at night.'*

And this story is very similar to one which originated in the quarters of the British Army stationed at Bergen-Belsen in Germany. It is a camp previously occupied by the S.S. in the

Second World War and close to the Concentration Camp of Belsen. Here a young girl does the tidying and the turning off of the radio. She was murdered by the S.S. so is it too much of a leap to wonder if our tidy person in Room 5 of the Old Post Office is the murdered girl in the cellar?

The final point about these premises is that they have been visited by the physic researchers who also found evidence of ghostly activity in Rooms 2 and 3 as well as the function room.

What of the connection between the murders in Milk Street and Bad Tom? For that we need to cross the narrow road to visit our next premises.

THE WHEATSHEAF PUBLIC HOUSE TOGETHER WITH NOS. 8 AND 8A MILK STREET

The Wheatsheaf public house which stands at the junction of

High Street and Milk Street has to be dealt together with the premises of the present day café at numbers 8 and 8a Milk Street. Both were once part of the same establishment dating from about 1617 and from the mid 1700s these Jacobean premises were

The Wheatsheaf.

known as a 'Riding House' offering both board and lodgings to travellers and the buying and selling of horses.

The premises are not only physically linked but they also share a number of ghostly inhabitants, although 'Bad Tom' whom we have referred to previously seems to prefer to remain in an upstairs room of the public house.

There is some talk that he may have been an accountant in his past life but one thing is for sure, he does not like younger people in general and has locked young female bar staff in the storeroom at the back of the premises. The temperature drops immediately by four degrees when he puts in an appearance. The licensee did manage to take a photograph once. This was on the first and only occasion he produced his camera when the temperature fell. The result was a pinprick – an orb – of light. The camera has failed to pick up anything since giving rise to speculation that Bad Tom now knows what a camera is and wants none of it.

Can we surmise that as we have an extremely bad spirit in Milk Street who does not like young people and has locked them into rooms that he was responsible for the deaths of the Davies children and Elspeth the young servant girl?

That is a huge leap without firm evidence, but you never know. It is possible.

Another ghost who confines herself to the Wheatsheaf is a woman known as the Grey Lady. She is a different ghost to the Grey Lady in the Lion Hotel. The Wheatsheaf lady is often seen walking through the crowded bar and leaves by the window which used to be a door.

Upsatirs in the old Riding House at 8 and 8A Milk Street.

The attached café at numbers 8 and 8a [presently Poppies] also has its own residents. There is a maid servant who lives in the room shown on page 35 and there are two children, a boy and a girl, playing on the stairs together whilst their grandmother waits nearby.

The young boy is playing happily but we do not know whether or not he is the same boy who makes a nuisance of himself in the Wheatsheaf. In the public house he will move things around as you watch. His favourite is a glass boot which moves of its own accord from one shelf to another behind the bar. He'll even spill your drink when no one is anywhere near it.

One ghost definitely shares the premises. He is Domas the coachman and is harmless. He has not been able to move on to the next world because of his love for a servant girl whom he has 'lost.' He is still looking for her and follows the females who go out into the rear yard to use the toilets. After following them to the loo he waits, occasionally trying to take a peek, before escorting them back across the yard. When he is around he is accompanied by a distinctive smell of smoke.

I was pleased to get some sort of confirmation about Domas, not only by a researcher but also by a lady who was taking a tour I was leading one evening. She had popped into the Wheatsheaf to use the facilities before we started and was amazed when the story was recounted to her. *'That is exactly what happened to me not thirty minutes ago,'* she exclaimed. *'I was that frightened I had to go and get my husband to stand outside the toilet whilst I was in there.'*

Coincidence? Do we really believe? But that night and only on that tour [so far] the overpowering smell of smoke arrived at every point we stopped at to talk. I like to think that Domas was taking a walk with us most likely because the lady on our tour reminded him so much of his lost love.

BELMONT

Belmont or Beautiful Hill heads down toward the thirteenth century Town Walls from Milk Street. It was built in 1701 and is the location of a version of one of the great, if fictitious, ghost stories of all time, that of *Christmas Carol* by Charles Dickens.

At the top of Belmont stands the wonderful Judges' Lodgings home to the High Court Judges when they visit Shrewsbury for the Crown Court sittings. The Crown Courts were formerly the Assizes and I wish I could tell you that the ghost of the infamous 'Hanging Judge,' Judge Jeffries who was educated at Shrewsbury School and continued to have associations with Shropshire was here with us. Alas he is not. His spirit now inhabits the body of a pig in Devon.

In 1984 Hollywood transformed the medieval streets and passages of Shrewsbury into a snow-covered Victorian London. The Judges' Lodgings became the home of Ebenezer Scrooge [George C. Scott played that part] where he was forced to confront the reality of his life by a succession of ghostly visitations. It was also on the first floor where Scrooge flung open the window on Christmas morning and shouted to a young lad to go and bring the largest prize turkey on sale in the market.

It was an incredibly good film version of the story and despite being fiction it is well worth a mention here.

THE OLD CHURCH OF ST CHAD

What remains of the original St Chad's Church stands directly opposite the Judges' Lodgings and incidentally was where the young lad was standing when he received his orders from Scrooge to go and get the turkey.

The church stands in a raised position on a natural hillock and once was outside the original town fortifications yet still protected in no small measure by the marshy ground which more or less surrounded it. Today it looks down into Milk Street and part of Princess Street several metres below.

All we are left with today since the church's collapse in the early hours of the 9 July, 1788 is the Lady Chapel but in its heyday the ancient Saxon church [one of four within the centre of Shrewsbury] was very large indeed attracting pilgrims to it from all over the land hoping to see a miracle or at least one of the thirty one religious relics in the martyrlogium.

At one stage the church was sending out into the countryside of Shropshire seventeen clergymen to spread the Word of God.

Today the shadows of the monks and priests still flit about the graveyard carrying out their duties. I would be puzzled to understand whether or not they are oblivious to the change of circumstances surrounding them in that the main body of the church is gone – at least I would be if it was not for the next ghost we are to meet. Here we have proof positive that they are inhabiting the world and the church they knew from all those centuries ago.

THE GOLDEN CROSS

The Golden Cross public house lies opposite the retaining wall of the grounds of Old St Chad's Church. It dates from 1428 and has held a liquor license since that time yet the upper rooms were once connected to the church by an enclosed gantry which stood about five metres above the ground level. The clergy used the rooms as a sacristy whilst the lay churchwardens used the gantry as an escape route to the pub when the sermon was going on too long.

The front bedroom of the Golden Cross overlooking the church is still visited by a monk wearing his habit. When he arrives there is a cold feeling in the room and a depression appears on the bed as though he is sitting on it. This monk has a sense of humour. The dressing table in the room stands on a floor which is not level due to the age of the premises and so items you would normally expect to find on such a piece of furniture often roll off. That may not be unusual but when our monk is about they roll off uphill!

One of the Holy Masses said in the church took place at 2.30 p.m. or 14.30 hours if you use the 24 hour clock. The date of the public house is 1428, which coincides with the time that a monk would have to leave the sacristy to reach his appointed place in the body of the church proper before the service began. And 14.28 or 2.28 p.m. is the exact time you might see our monk hurrying from the bedroom and across the now lost gantry. Only he is five metres in the air. The monk disappears half way across the street as if he is reaching the church having left the overhead passageway.

Are the dates and times just a coincidence?

In 2008 we had a newly reported phenomenon. Guests who were staying overnight in the upstairs bedrooms of the Golden Cross were being woken in the early hours by the sounds of an exuberant street sweeper wielding a stiff yard broom who was cleaning the 'shut' or passage below their windows.

Night after night this continued and they took some convincing that the local council's street cleaners were not as diligent as to be working at that hour, so the next night when the broom began to sweep once more the guests got up and looked out of the window. The noise continued but there was no one [alive] in the passageway.

Before we leave this location we need to recount what happened when the church collapsed that early morning in the July of 1788.

Immediately after the collapse the people who lived in the area left their homes and headed for the scene of destruction. They had one thought in their mind – to protect the Norman font which was now exposed to the open air. A guard was mounted to *secure it against the acts of witches.'*

Whereas the last witch in England had been executed in the 1740s there is no doubt that ordinary people still believed in them and the power they had. It was all too recent in their memory. The value of the font lay in the Holy Water which it had contained for any such water applied to the lips of innocent girls would ensure that no man would be able to refrain from kissing them. I think that is the nice eighteenth century way of saying that the unfortunate young girl would be procured for prostitution.

And witches have been identified as still being present at our next location.

PRINCESS STREET [or CANDLE LANE]

About fifty metres away and easily visible from the Golden Cross public house, a fourteenth century building stands at the junction of College Hill and Princess Street. Yet again we have had a name change to a street, the evocatively named Candle Lane being replaced by Princess Street after the visit of Princess Victoria to the town before her accession to the throne.

The building is presently occupied by a bookshop with a rather nice tearoom attached to it, the tearoom being located fully in Princess Street.

Physic researchers have certainly identified that witches are active in the old building.

I like the name Candle Lane as it was the place where religious pilgrims visiting Old St Chad's Church would stop to buy their candles to light before the altar. It is yet another coincidence that this street is the one which has suffered more from fire during the history of the town than any other.

In the timber-framed building on the corner four children were burned to death on the upper floor whilst their mother died of smoke inhalation on the stairs trying to reach them.

This was in the 1500s but even today, during the summer months, the people who work in either shop or café can smell smoke and hear children playing upstairs.

In a separate incident a maid hung herself from one of the beams and is seen suspended above the floor begging for the peace she so wants.

As tragic as these events were the most worrying aspect of the building is the ghost which actually physically strikes visitors in the centre of the back. It usually takes place as someone climbs the stairs.

I used to think that maybe it was the ghost of Elizabeth Bickerstaff who was murdered hereabouts in the August of 1551 and then chopped up before being buried under the floor. Her kinsman, Thomas, was responsible although he thought he would be clever and report her missing. Unfortunately for him the landlord's dog dug up her remains a few weeks later. So maybe Lizzie was getting her own back.

However I have since discovered that being struck on the torso is the way in which an evil and malevolent spirit passes on evil to another. I wish I knew who all the people were who have been struck. I for one would like to follow it up and see if anything bad had happened to them after the attack.

COLLEGE HILL

College Hill takes its name from the fact that it abuts the grounds of Old St Chad's Church that church being a colleg-iate church. In other words it sent out the clergy to preach.

Today the street contains a convent which is a nice continuity of use connecting us to the past as the priests of St Chad's used to live along this quiet thoroughfare.

There are two properties which are haunted along, or just off, College Hill.

THE APOTHECARY'S HOUSE

The Apothecary's House is found at number 12 College Hill and dates from the sixteenth century. Here we have something unpleasant happening. Electrical items will turn themselves on and off [just like the juke box in the Nag's Head we visited earlier] but also something much more worrying.

The daughter of the occupants once told me this story.

Her mother and father were asleep in the bedroom of their home and both woke up at the same time. Nothing unusual in that but they found that they could not move or speak and had this tingling feeling all over their bodies.

'It was as if they were being starved of oxygen but once they forced themselves to move the feeling left them immediately. I think something could have been trying to suffocate them.'

COFFEE HOUSE PASSAGE

Coffee House Passage is a narrow alleyway leading from College Hill to the Market Square of Shrewsbury. It takes its name from the fact that it runs down the side of the Music Hall, formerly the thirteenth century hall of Sir William Vaughan, and since its re-vamp in the early 1800s the wealthy men of the town would meet in the building to read the newspapers, play cards, listen to lectures and take coffee.

Just inside the passage as you enter from the Market Square is a carved beam above our heads. The date is inscribed upon the wood together with the initials of the carpenter, *'1577 GP.'* There is a door but a few feet away from the engraved beam which gives access to a lovingly-restored first floor ladies' dress shop by means of a staircase dating from 1713.

The present owners were blissfully unaware of the tragedy which took place in their premises when a young woman was found hanging from a beam. We chatted amiably on that first floor the owners happy to take a break from their renovations and decorating work as they returned the place to its former glory. Only whilst we spoke the temperature around me took a distinct tumble and for an instant I was certain that I caught a fleeting glimpse of something at about head height. The feeling was so brief that I could not be sure what I had seen or felt, but I was certain that we were standing directly beneath 'the spot.'

I thought it better not to mention their resident ghost and left, but do visit the shop if for nothing else than to admire Shrewsbury at its eighteenth-century finest.

Further into the passage a building juts out narrowing the 'shut' considerably. This was the town's police station between 1845 and 1853. It was here in the July of 1846 that two fat geese that had been found wandering were brought for safe keeping. The Town Crier broadcast the find but as no one came forward to claim their property the landlord of a nearby public house was asked to come and buy them for the table. He arrived but too late. The cops had eaten the geese.

I have not myself experienced these two very noisy birds although I was told by an old constable that they could be heard making *'a right old racket'* on occasions – although just once I thought I had. Unfortunately it was 1984 and the squawking geese were no more than 'props' wandering about in the nearby Market Square where they were being used to good effect by the movie makers of a 'Christmas Carol' re-creating an 'authentic' nineteenth century Christmas market.

Ah well!

THE GHOSTS
OF THE
WELSH WARD

B Y THE time I arrived in Shrewsbury in 1969 the Welsh
Ward or 'Frankwell' had been extended for policing pur-
poses to include the western part of the town of Shrewsbury
within the loop of the river. Frankwell itself lies, as it always
has, on the far bank of the Severn as the river loops around
the town and since Saxon times has been a place *'beyond the
pale.'*

The Saxon invaders of England forced the indigenous population ever westwards towards Wales and the new-comers'
language reflected their view of their world. From the Saxon
the word *'Welsh'* meant *'foreigner'* whilst the word *'Mercia,'* the
local kingdom [today the name of the local police force is the
West Mercia] stood for *'boundary.'* One of their street names
found in this ward is 'The Mardol' meaning the *'Devil's
Boundary.'*

The Welsh Bridge [also once known as St George's Bridge]
connects the notorious suburb to the town itself. However
despite this physical connection the passing of time did little
to alter the reputation of Frankwell or the Welsh Ward. By the
early 1820s the area was described as, *'The main haunt of gangs*

of offenders and their abettors who infest the town pilfering from honest tradesmen. These noxious vermin run to these "hole-and-corner" boroughs for refuge when pursued.' And another description: *'Whole rows of houses are tenanted by shameless and wretched females to which thieves and robbers are traced.'*

ST AUSTIN'S FRIARS

These white friars [Augustinians] so called because of the colour of their robes arrived in Shrewsbury in 1250 A.D. and set up their monastery on an old burial and marshy piece of ground just to the right of the present day Welsh Bridge on the town side. The area is now dominated by a number of restaurants in rather pleasantly renovated industrial buildings overlooking the river.

In one of these buildings, the last one before the Quarry Park, highly coloured spheres or orbs of light have been seen appearing above the heads of numerous diners. Sadly there is no information at all to indicate the identity of the person the energy source relates to. I like to think it could be Isoloda, a fourteenth century anchoress or female hermit who used to live in wretched conditions in this area. Maybe she is making up for her frugal lifestyle now enjoying some of the good things in life. Or maybe it could be one of the *'poor women of Frankwell'* who used to come to this very spot long before the industrial premises were built here to wash the clothes of those rich enough to pay the penny a load.

The truth is we have no idea who the poor soul is – but maybe we should rejoice that whoever it is has found his or her own place of solace just as close to water as it is possible to get.

THE MARDOL

Prior to the new Welsh Bridge being built in the late 1700s access to the fortified town of Shrewsbury from the west would have been by crossing between the towers of the old bridge and entering at the foot of the Mardol.

A few yards from that point we find our first haunted premises.

THE KING'S HEAD PUBLIC HOUSE

This building dates from the 1300s and was once known as 'The Last Inn.'

Again we hark back to Saxon imagery. Mardol – the devil's boundary: The Last Inn – it is as if we are at the point where civilization is coming to an end.

The public house is rightly famous for its wall painting dating from somewhere between the mid 1400s and early 1500s and which remained hidden until 1987. One fact which I find quite startling is that for such a historic area this is the only building in the immediate vicinity where I've discovered the existence of active ghosts.

The front bedroom above the street is cold in just one place and 'a presence' is detected standing in the corner of the corridor outside that same room. The licensee has never felt threatened by this visitor – *'It is just there,'* she says.

In the bar downstairs there is another presence. We believe it is a different ghost to the upstairs one as this time when it appears a warm feeling pervades the space around it. And the downstairs ghost has a sense of humour. An old and treasured framed photograph of the family's previous generations stands proudly on the wall behind the bar. It is moved time after time and carefully placed on the floor on the public side of the serving counter. It is impossible for the photograph to travel the two metres without help and in any event it is carefully placed on the floor being treated gently and with respect.

ROUSHILL

Off to the left hand side of Mardol as you walk toward the town centre there is a wide and steep pathway used by pedestrians. This is Roushill. At the top of the incline we have two separate ghosts.

The first is a dairy maid who was accused of watering down the milk she was selling. She is not happy at being called a 'cheat' as she mutters her denials to all she meets. I think it very strange that such a small thing could prevent her spirit from finding rest. If she'd been falsely accused of being one of the sixty or so prostitutes who lived in the area during the mid to late 1800s then maybe I could understand it better. But there it is.

After giving a talk recently in the Shrewsbury area I was approached by a man who told me of a 'new' ghost. At least it was a new one to me.

He was first seen in 1947 by the mechanic father of my informant. His dad was on the way home down Roushill one dark January night with his head bowed into the snow which was being blown about by a keen wind when he literally bumped into a police constable.

He apologised as he moved aside and walked on. However, after a couple of metres he stopped as realisation dawned that the policeman had not moved an inch. Not only that but the officer was not wearing a winter coat [greatcoat] and the uniform was all wrong. The jacket was one of those nineteenth century types with the silver buttons fastened all the way up to his chin. If that wasn't enough he wore a top hat not a helmet.

[Helmets were not introduced until about 1863 so the ghost is quite old.]

As he looked back at the unmoving officer he could only watch as the figure gently faded into nothing.

HILL'S LANE

To the right hand side of the Mardol as you take your leave of the river is Hill's Lane.

The crowning glory of that area is Rowley's House which was built in the early 1600s by William Rowley who was a rich cloth merchant. It was the first building in Shrewsbury to be built of brick and for a long time it was hidden amongst the slum tenements, factories and foundries which had grown up about it.

ROWLEY'S HOUSE

Rowley's House has two ghosts sharing the building which has been variously used over the last three hundred and odd years as a factory, storehouse, oil depot and a town museum. The first ghost is that of a lady dressed in fine clothes who has been seen resting on a bed upstairs. The bed was an exhibit in the museum. It is thought likely that she may have died on the bed in childbirth as she has also been seen in the house from which the four-poster bed came to be donated.

The other ghost is that of a man who wanders the corridors and has been seen by various people who have either lived in or worked on the premises. He has been reported as being *'at peace'* and *'not frightening'* and does not seem to have any connection with the female ghost. He just ignores her and was certainly seen long before the exhibit with its attendant female ghost arrived.

* * * * *

There is one ghost who wanders **Hill's Lane** and the area in the immediate vicinity of Rowley's House. Today the area is given over to car parks and is light and airy with trees here and there but no doubt the nineteenth century was very different with numerous alleyways or shuts in amongst the slums hereabouts. It was not the most pleasant of places with people and buildings being crammed in on top of one another. The 1861 census gives us an idea of the type of people living here, pedlars, drovers, weavers, cutlery grinders, a Welsh tailor, an army pensioner who was Irish and one Assam Ali from Mecca, *'a vendor of tracts.'*

The area had not changed much by the June of 1886. At this time we find the 37 year old William Mabbot, a married man with three children being in the employment of a grocer who had a shop near to Rowley's House.

Rowley's House.

William was sent to Welshpool some 15 miles away to sell some of his master's produce at a fair which was being held there. He was also instructed that he may as well collect some money which was owed to his employer by a man called William Samuels. Mabbot succeeded in getting most of the debt paid off and was no doubt feeling pleased with himself. He accepted the pint of porter offered to him by Samuels but within thirty minutes of taking a good swig he was dead. His porter had been poisoned.

Now a forlorn figure in the dress of a working man from the nineteenth century walks Hill's Lane and the alleyways which are now long gone. He's a sad man – no doubt looking for his wife, his children and his lost life.

HOLLINGS HOUSE, 35 HILL'S LANE

This old building over four storeys certainly has the façade of one dating from the end of the 1700s but stands on the site of one which was much, much older. The ground floor is given over to shop premises whilst a family lives on the floors above.

The family has had a long association with the premises, certainly since the time when it was a tobacco wholesaler up until the 1970s. I mention that time frame as there was no reported ghostly activity until fairly recently.

One evening the gentleman of the house was at the top of the building working in his study. He was alone apart from his dog which faithfully snoozed away at his master's feet and he remembers how quiet everything was. It was a still night with no wind and no sounds from the town reached his ears. It was then that he heard some doors opening and closing on that attic floor. The hackles on his dog's neck rose immediately and it was obviously distressed before bolting down the stairs.

The owner was not long in following, pausing only long enough to make sure that the doors could not have been opening and closing as they were all firmly secured in the open position against the walls.

This defied any logical explanation until a few nights later. Once more he was working in his study but on this occasion a woman appeared in the room. In his words, *'She was like a solid shadow. Like a negative but you could not see through her. She was possibly a Victorian lady as she was wearing a bustle under her skirts. She came up behind me and touched my rear trouser pocket.'*

The person who experienced this is a solid and respected member of the community and there is no doubt as to what he saw and felt although he has no logical explanation for it all.

I just wonder if the recent disturbance at Rowley's House only some fifty metres away has prompted some action. The Town Museum presently housed in Rowley's is closing down before a move to new premises. Could the ghostly lady on the bed exhibit have been disturbed and is looking for somewhere else to lay her head? Both ghosts are from the same period of 'bustles beneath dresses' and the one in Hollings House has only just appeared – at about the same time of the proposed move out of Rowley's House.

Is it coincidence or something more? You can choose.

THE GHOSTS OF THE WELSH WARD

MARDOL HEAD

At the top of the incline away from the river the Mardol comes to an end at a place called Mardol Head which is now dominated by a piece of modern sculpture called 'Darwin's Gate.' Here we find the Hole in the Wall public house which has a dark and dank passageway leading off to the right hand side and back of the building. Today it is called Drayton's Passage and is the first 'shut' to have a record of the people who used to live in it. These were the Schutte family in the late 1200s. There are blocks of sandstone around the side doorway to the public house which date from 1325. In recent years the Hole in the Wall has been extended to incorporate another licensed premises which stood right next door to it – the Blood Tub.

This building activity seems to have disturbed the spirit of a young girl called Sarah Schutte. She was a lady-in-waiting to the influential Charlton family in the early 1300s and who lived nearby.

Was it a coincidence that our ghostly Sarah made herself known to a barmaid who was also called Sarah? Barmaid Sarah left soon after the meeting.

Sarah Schutte has never found rest after dying in tragic circumstances. She had taken a lover only, just as in Romeo and Juliet, the boy came from a family in the town with whom the powerful Charltons [and therefore their employees, the Schuttes] had something of a feud going on.

The two lovers used to meet in the graveyard of [now 'Old'] St Chad's but when Sarah's family found out it was curtains for her. They could not afford to offend the Charltons so they locked their daughter in the cellar below the 'shut' and starved her to death.

Now Sarah Schutte turns up after the customers have gone home walking through a wall which was not there in her time.

THE MARKET SQUARE

Drayton's Passage and the nearby Gullet Passage lead from Mardol Head and Shoplatch into the Market Square of Shrewsbury.

The Square has been the main market for the town since the King's Market in the centre of Saxon Shrewsbury which we are yet to visit became too small in the early 1200s. The Market Square is dominated by the centrally positioned Old Market Hall dating from 1596 and surrounded by buildings which represent just about every period in history from the thirteenth century to the 1960s. Despite nearly 800 years of constant use there are only a few ghosts in the immediate area that we know much about.

One restaurant/café on the eastern side of the Square reports *'something unpleasant'* in the basement and the staff do not like going in there. The premises stand on the site of the Old Shirehall which used to house the Assize and Quarter Sessions courts in the past, so maybe the cellars were cells once upon a time and the unpleasantness comes from a prisoner incarcerated there. But we are merely guessing here.

The Music Hall stands on the site of, and incorporates parts of, the thirteenth-century Vaughan's Mansion. It is presently an entertainment venue with plans to turn it into a large museum. On closing for the night, sometimes late if there has been a production or play on, the staff will lock up as you would expect before heading for their cars. Only sometimes as they drive away they will see that the lights have come back on inside the building even though no one can possibly be on the premises.

I like to think that the culprit is *'Poor Edith'* who was once a servant of the Vaughans and who died a horrible death in the building all those centuries ago. She had fallen into a vat of boiling liquor and although rescued she lay in great pain for fifteen days before she perished of her scalds.

Maybe she needs a bit of light relief by turning the lights on and off.

Finally, when the Market Hall was being constructed a young child was crushed to death by a falling beam. These beams are indeed immense and are easily viewed today.

Once when I was a constable on night duty I walked and walked my beat, doubling back again and again. I could hear a child crying constantly and knew something was amiss. The crying carried on for at least two hours – as did my fruitless search. I never seemed to get any closer to the noise. But back then in the late 1960s, I knew nothing of the crushed girl.

HIGH STREET

Walking east out of The Square along the High Street there is a shop premises clearly identified as 'Number 41.'

Back in the October of 1960 the premises were a butcher's shop called Longford and Davies. It became infamous for one thing. The last person to be hanged in Shrewsbury worked at the shop.

No one has any idea who the ghost is who can be found in the back storeroom of Number 41. One female member of staff certainly came face-to-face with a man. The room has always been colder than it should and, although alone in there, the same lady has been touched lightly on the shoulder more than once. But it was the face that made the most indelible impression.

I use the words face-to-face deliberately as all that appeared in front of her was the face of a young man with short dark hair. *'He had no body just the face and he was peering at me as if he was looking around a corner. Only there is no corner there to look around.'*

Who the young man with the short dark hair is, is anyone's guess.

PRIDE HILL

Heading north from the Market Square is the main pedestrianized shopping area of the town known as Pride Hill. Despite most of the buildings of today looking as if they are from the eighteenth century the thoroughfare is a very old one dating back to the time the town was founded by Alfred the Great. It was named after the Pride family, rich merchants from the 1200s. The premises on the left side of the incline all stand on the original town walls, the building of which began in the 1220s. Incidentally the best view of the old walls can be found downstairs in McDonalds.

Practically every shop has something to tell the enquirer, whether it is of eerie feelings, coldness and temperature drops or not wanting to enter any of the underground passages which criss-cross the busy thoroughfare above, so we will confine ourselves to the more 'interesting' apparitions and happenings.

NUMBER 4 PRIDE HILL

Number 4 stands at the foot of the incline and next to the premises which house the remains of Bennett's Hall [1250 – 1260]. Things got so bad in the shop with the unruly Victorian gentleman *'playing up'* that his spirit had to be exorcised.

NUMBER 16 PRIDE HILL

The staff of the mobile phone company which currently uses these premises were working late one night in the December of 2007 when one of them took some catalogues to the basement.

He felt a chill draft and looked to see where it was coming from but all he saw was *'something'* which stood between him and the wall totally obscuring his vision. He dropped his load and ran. The staff have always called their cellar *'the dungeon'* and this incident, along with *'something on the stairs'* has convinced them that their guests were hanged on this part of the old town walls.

They are young men on the staff but now they do not use their toilet any more. It is in the dungeon so they go to McDonalds instead.

NUMBER 40 PRIDE HILL

This is one of the oldest surviving buildings in Shrewsbury and presently occupied by a well known sweet shop. They have an easy going spirit whom they've nicknamed *'Friendly Fred'* even though chocolates do sometimes end up on the floor.

NUMBERS 28 – 29 PRIDE HILL

28 and 29 are to be found near the top of Pride Hill close to The Cross. Presently it is occupied by a national retailer of men's clothing. Staff members are well aware of not only a ghost upstairs but another in the cellar. Unfortunately for the spirit downstairs the cellar often floods due to the fact that they know the shop sits atop a long forgotten 'Witches Well.' The cold, damp and frequently very wet cellar is a far cry from the magical qualities once attributed to such wells but there is a spirit of a witch nearby and known by the name of Bertha.

W.H. SMITH, PRIDE HILL

Bertha the witch inhabits the newsagents, W.H.Smith. The building they now occupy has had a long history since the time the Pride family themselves owned it back in the 1200s. It has also been used as a grocery store and famous tearoom which held tea dances before the current owners took over.

Bertha is a beautiful young lady who stares down from the first floor 'Battle of Shrewsbury' window and appears to be staring at the Pride Hill Cross, the principal place of execution for prisoners in days' gone-by. Certainly David, the last 'real' Prince of Wales was executed at this spot by hanging, drawing and quartering.

Many, many others died here and so it is assumed that Bertha is looking down watching as a loved one leaves this earth in a most unpleasant fashion.

Bertha is still active. If you see her, and she is always around somewhere even on a busy Saturday, she has the nasty habit of decaying before your eyes.

The manager had a strange experience with the ghost fairly recently. He was in the stockroom on the first floor doing a stock take. The building was locked up and he was alone.

However whilst he was busy something struck him in the middle of the back causing him to whip round. The only thing out of place was the plastic top off a cheap biro pen which was now lying on the floor where it most certainly had not been a few moments earlier. He checked around and found a single pen in a box of such pens on a shelf some three metres away but unlike all the others in the box, this one particular pen was without its plastic top.

THE OLD POST OFFICE BUILDING ON PRIDE HILL

Directly opposite W.H. Smith and the Pride Hill Cross is a modern looking building [above Numbers 28 and 29] which used to be the post office at the beginning of the twentieth century. A soldier of the First World War sits in there waiting for a letter to arrive which would give him an exemption from going to the war in the trenches. The letter never arrived from London and he left with his regiment only to be killed in action. He is still there – and still waiting for that life-saving letter.

70 STEPS

The 70 Steps is one of three remaining breaches in the ancient town walls of Shrewsbury which allowed the people living inside the fortified town access to the meadows and the river far below. These steps stand near to the entrance of the modern day shopping precinct and against one-time licensed premises once known as 'The Disorderly House.'

This tale dates from sometime between the First and Second World Wars. A number of police constables paraded for night duty at their police station in Swan Hill and were given their duties for their shift. At 10 p.m. they left on foot patrol of the town. One such constable was in his late twenties, had dark hair and was in full health as one would expect from men walking up to twenty miles a night.

But on this night that particular constable failed to meet

his sergeant at the appointed time and place, something which did not happen unless there was a serious problem. A search began for the missing man and eventually he was found half way down the 70 Steps. Unfortunately he was now hardly recognisable. His hair had turned white, his eyes were wide and staring and he babbled and salivated uncontrollably. No one ever found out what he had seen to turn him from a normal man into such a wreck in no more than a couple of hours for he spent the rest of his life in a mental institution.

Could it have been the work of witches? After all we know that if you annoy a witch they have the power to curse you with the 'evil eye' – and witches are but yards from the 70 Steps.

THE GHOSTS
OF THE
CASTLE WARD

TO THE NORTH the River Severn almost completes its protective and encircling loop around the town of Shrewsbury. It is on this narrow neck of land, maybe only a couple of hundred metres wide, that the first defensive works were thrown up by Alfred the Great. There is nothing to prove that he did choose this very place but as the purpose of his defensive 'burghs' was to provide a safe place so that the law, church and trade could flourish, he could not have chosen better.

Certainly with the Norman Invasion the occupiers who reached Shrewsbury in about 1067 A.D. took over that ideal defensive position to begin over two hundred years of serious work on the castle itself.

The castle dominated the northern approach to the town looking down from its mount to the Foregate, a rough and ready area which by the nineteenth century was described as, *'It abounds with lodging houses in which a miserable class of vagabond without means of honest subsistence are constantly housed.'*

SHREWSBURY CASTLE

Today, the castle is the best preserved Conquest Castle in the country.

Within a couple of years of the Normans arriving in the town the men of Shropshire, Chester and Wales were in revolt against them and laid siege to the castle. And this is the time from which we have three ghost stories to talk of.

The leader of the insurrection at Shrewsbury was a man called 'Wild Edric' but although attacks on other Norman strongholds such as Hereford had proved successful, Shrewsbury held out against his forces.

Some say Edric was bought off but whatever the truth was his own side were none-too-happy. They imprisoned him with some of his men in the disused Roman lead mines about twenty kilometres south of the town. His ghost and that of his band of horsemen, now known locally as *'The Old Men'*, are allowed out of their underground prison only when danger threatens the country. At these times the armed riders charge across the South Shropshire moorland hills blowing their horns. Edric is unmistakable on his white charger.

This 'hunt' has been witnessed. The first time it was recorded was just before the outbreak of the Crimean War in the mid 1800s when a miner and his daughter saw the sight near the village of Minsterley. It has been witnessed by others immediately before the Boer War in 1899 and the First World War. An old neighbour of mine also told me he saw the ghostly 'hunt' near the tiny village of Bentlawnt in the South Shropshire Hills in 1939.

One further ghost story involving Wild Edric is that during the twelve days of Christmas he is allowed out from his underground prison but only in the shape of a great black dog which roams the hills.

I have confirmation from a friend and neighbour who was out shooting on Boxing Day one year on the Stapeley Moor when he came across *'a huge black leopard'* which seemed quite surprised to see him and promptly disappeared with a low growl.

* * * * *

The second ghost from the eleventh century involves Shrewsbury's one and only serial killer. His name was Bloudy [or Bloody] Jack.

Some say he was deranged by the arrival of the Normans who began to tear down parts of the town to make the area more defensible but what we do know is that he was seen dragging a girl called 'Fanny' by the hair toward the castle. The townspeople were roused and arrived in time to save the girl from a terrible fate and caught Jack who was trying to hide in a chimney. They searched the building and found eight complete sets of fingers and toes in a box. These were his trophies taken from previous victims whilst they were still alive.

The missing girls' bodies were never found. They had either been put in the river or the pigs ate them.

The townspeople cut off Jack's head and stuck it on a pole, but his spirit still wanders the area of the castle. We will return to that in a moment.

* * * * *

The third and final ghost only appears during a storm which is so violent that only the devil himself could have conjured it up. The story dates from about 1080 – 1090 A.D. when Roger de Montgomery, a kinsman of William the Conqueror, was in charge of Shrewsbury Castle. Roger was a religious man responsible for bringing the Benedictine monks to Shrewsbury to construct the Abbey of St Peter and St Paul and in fact became a monk three days before he died in 1094.

It was to Shrewsbury Castle and Roger de Montgomery that Adeliza of Normandy came during a wild storm. The storm had come upon her party and she had a vision that their lives would only be spared if a church would be built on that spot where she'd received her visitation. [Quatford near Bridgnorth in Shropshire.] She agreed and made her way to Shrewsbury Castle to find De Montgomery and ask for his help in realising her promise. Only the devil knew about it and had no intention of letting Christianity spread even further a-field and so conjured up the storm to end all storms to try and prevent her from reaching her goal.

The devil failed and the church was built but if a huge storm hits the town then be prepared to see Adeliza and her party fighting their way through the atrocious conditions toward the safety of Shrewsbury Castle.

CASTLE STREET – THE OUTER BAILEY

St Nicholas Presbyterian Church was built in 1870 but has now been turned into a commercial premises stretching over three floors. However the nineteenth century church building was built on the site of an original Norman church which stood within the outer bailey of the castle and it is to this church that Bloudy Jack still makes his way. He bangs on the main door to the building demanding entry which makes me wonder if he had tried to escape the angry mob by trying to claim sanctuary.

That may not be too fanciful as when the current occupiers of the building did some renovation work prior to opening for business they found they had four Christian ghosts residing there. The two men and two women exude a *'nice feeling'* and perhaps it was those who kept Bloudy Jack at bay so he could receive his just deserts. Who knows?

However, at least one of our Christian ghosts has a sense of humour. The business trades over three floors and there is a till on each. At the end of one particular day's trading the cash boxes were collected and placed on the bottom step of the staircase. No one else was in the building and the door locked. The lady was busy on the ground floor when she heard the sound of metal falling and thinking that somehow or other someone was tampering with the cash boxes she headed for the staircase. She found the containers had not been moved but the cash had been taken out of them and neatly lined up.

I think the Christian ghosts also had a hand in the next story.

My wife and I were friendly with an elderly lady whom we used to meet most mornings for a coffee in town. It was her grandfather and uncle who made the small round window right at the top of the church and positioned it above the main door. It must be all of twenty metres up on the building.

This was not long after the turn of the twentieth century and so they had no option but to use two long ladders, one placed on either side of the prepared hole and then carry the heavy window up between them. They got to the top when an almighty gust of wind came and blew the window out of their

Home to our four Christian ghosts.

hands. Imagine their relief when the window was blown right into the hole and into the perfect position.

You might say that was a miracle or, on the other hand you may think the Christian ghosts are still guarding this Holy place.

CASTLE COURT

Still within the old boundary of the outer bailey is Castle Court which once contained not only the Old Police House but also the entrance to the Old Gaol dating from 1705. Entry into the courtyard is gained by walking up a narrow 'shut' beneath a building which arches over the walkway.

Castle Court.

To the right of the courtyard is the Old Police House and entrance to the Old Gaol. It was the building out of which the Night Watch would come to patrol the town before the advent of paid police constables. However, it was in the late nineteenth century that a constable did hang himself in the building but we know that he changed his mind before he died. When he appears dangling above the floor he has his hands between the rope and his neck as he tries in vain to stop himself choking to death.

On the other side of the courtyard is a building which has been converted into apartments. When this was a business premises a poltergeist used to throw things across the room with rolls of sellotape and a metal hole-punch being the favourite weapons of choice.

CASTLE FOREGATE

The magnificent nineteenth century railway station lies in the shadow of the castle perched on its high mound and is the home to one ghost who is to be found on Platform 3.

In the late 1880s a Shrewsbury councillor was sitting in his horse drawn carriage waiting for a train to arrive. It was snowing very heavily and he must have been getting quite worried by the lateness of the train and would welcome a quick return home to be spared from the elements.

Unfortunately for him he was never to get home. The weight of the snow brought down the station's cast iron and glass roof and he was crushed to death. He is still in the station on Platform 3 near to the Castle Street entrance and still alternating glances between the pocket watch he holds in his hand and the empty railway line.

The horse escaped.

* * * * *

Near to the railway station toward the bottom of Castle Street stands the town's lovely reference library. Just below this building there is a small shop. This location would have meant that the premises were just inside the Castle Foregate entrance to the outer bailey.

This small shop, currently a whole-food retailer, had a poltergeist which they disturbed when the place was being fitted out to accommodate the new business. This seems to be one factor quite common in the spirit world. They seem more likely to appear when their surroundings are disturbed.

In this case the mischief was very little although just enough to alert the staff that something wasn't quite right. A packet of sultanas would fall to the floor when no one was anywhere near it. I dare say there are plenty of logical explanations for that but how do we explain that it was always sultanas and always from exactly the same place?

CASTLE STREET

The Raven Hotel, once a coaching inn, used to stand proudly on Castle Street but alas the planners had their way and replaced the historic building with a modern structure which now houses Marks and Spencer's.

Castle Street effortlessly joins Pride Hill and like all the premises on the right hand side of both those thoroughfares

Castle Street today.

as you walk away from the castle, the Raven used to stand on the original town walls dating from the early 1200s.

There is but one ghost associated with the building now occupied by Marks and Spencer. Before the last renovations there was a staircase leading from the ground floor down to a lower sales floor. People using these stairs would be physically jostled even though there was no one around.

Since the last renovations in about 2006 when that staircase was removed, I have had no reports of any other apparition within the premises. Outside is a different matter but we will return to that in due course.

3 CASTLE STREET

These premises are currently occupied by a games shop and sit on the old town walls. In 1876 number three was owned by E.R. Davies, a jeweller in the town.

The current shop premises will look per-fectly normal to the twenty-first century customer but not many will know that there is a trap door secreted beneath their feet. Down below are tunnels which once

The author exploring.

allowed servants inconspicuous access to the full length of the buildings in the immediate vicinity including the sadly missed Raven Hotel [M&S] and the old tea rooms belonging to Morris and Company [W.H. Smith].

It does not take a lot of imagination to see white coated waiters with silver platters or the Victorian serving girls in their black dresses with white pinafores and caps. But the ghosts are much older.

Upstairs there is a man who stays in this world only because of the love he had for Bertha the witch girl whom we have already met in the previous chapter. Did she cast a spell over him?

The other is that of a child who is still very active playing hide and seek and running up and down the stairs. Many a time a member of staff has been passed on the stairs by a child in a hurry.

TRAITOR'S GATE ALSO KNOWN AS ST MARY'S WATER LANE

As we leave the castle behind and return toward the centre of Shrewsbury along Castle Street, the first turning to the left leads eventually to the lovely old leafy square around St Mary's Church.

However, within a few yards of Castle Street we come firstly to a wonderful old house called Perches House after John Perch, a shearman and four times bailiff of the town who enlarged the original house dating from the early part of the fifteenth century. His work took place in 1581 after he bought the place for forty three pounds and ten shillings. It is a perfect example of a building constructed by what is called 'close studding.' Back in John's time wood, especially oak, was in short supply as most of it was being gobbled up by the Royal Navy but he used as much wood as he could get hold of. It has been suggested that you could remove nearly three quarters of the wood and the house would still be sound. In other words he was showing everyone just how rich he was.

By 1624 the house was in the hands of a barrister-at-law called Timothy Turner who is described as *'a nasty piece of work.'* He had eleven legitimate children [two of whom were sons] by three different wives as well as a whole host of illegitimate ones sired on a succession of his maid servants who had been unlucky enough to find employment with him.

His two sons were Tim, *'a daddy's boy'* and a royalist who purchased a knighthood from Charles II for somewhere in the region of £700, and Tom who was not on good terms with his father because of his father's dalliances outside of wedlock. Tom was later killed in action fighting for the Parliamentary forces at Lilleshall in Shropshire. It was also Tom who was thought to be the 'traitor' who opened the gates in the Norman archway at the bottom of St Mary's Water Lane to let Cromwell's forces take the town.

One of the girls employed by Timothy Turner the elder had an illegitimate child which lived for only a couple of days after being born. Then the servant girl died a few days later. Rumours ran wild: Suicide? Murder?

One thing for certain was that the vicar made sure the entry of death in the church records did not read as this rich

Perches House.

family would have wanted the deaths recorded. The church-
man may not have wanted to delve too much into the circumstances of the deaths but there was sufficient doubt in his
mind to endorse the records as *'not plague victims.'*

Does this mean that Turner the elder suggested that this is what carried mother and child off but the vicar had too much of a conscience to go along whole-heartedly with one of the richest and most powerful men in the town?

To this day both mother and child are in the house. The baby cries a lot and mum is seen trying to comfort the infant.

ST MARY'S SHUT AND LITTLE SHUT

Another way to approach St Mary's Church from Castle Street is to take the two tiny and narrow alleyways. Once upon a time the two alleyways or 'shuts' were one but are now separated by an open area used as a car park. This open area has two known ghosts.

The first is a criminal, a pick-pocket who stands in the corner of the yard just waiting for a potential victim. When you bear in mind that this area was once slum housing of the very worst kind, then he is no longer out of place.

The second is a ghost I met on the evening of my first ever Ghost Tour of the town which I take on behalf of the town council and is the ghostly activity outside the Raven Hotel [now Marks and Spencer] I referred to earlier. I always walk the proposed route of the tours I take to make sure everything is in order and this ghostly interaction took place during that activity.

The town was deserted and the dark streets as quiet as the grave. No one was in the area of St Mary's or in Castle Street. There was not even the noise of a motor vehicle anywhere to break the silence. I walked through Little Shut which actually goes through a dwelling house for a few metres and then I emerged into the car parking area. All of a sudden I was being followed by a 'lady-of-the-night' dressed in 1940s style and clip-clopping along in her high heels. She had even got tea-stained legs to make it look as though she was wearing stockings with a rough darker line drawn down the back of her calf muscles. Her lipstick was thickly applied.

Of course I have no proof because no one [alive] was anywhere around. I walked on quickening my pace and as I disappeared into the second alleyway she stopped and did not follow. The shut emerges onto Castle Street directly opposite where the Raven Hotel used to stand.

It was only later that I found out the Raven had been the headquarters for the American Army stationed in Shropshire. I now believe that this prostitute from the Second World War is still in the alleyways touting for business from the troops.

As this lady is a relatively 'new' or unknown ghost before my meeting with her, a meeting which more or less coincided with the time Marks and Spencer were undergoing refurbishment and moving the previous staircase from its original position, maybe she has moved outside.

There have been no reported incidents of 'jostling' on the stairs since the refurbishment – which is not surprising as they are no longer there and our lady-of-the-night has appeared in the alleyway directly opposite. I don't know. Maybe she moved from inside the Raven to the place she took her customers. I will let you decide.

ST MARY'S PLACE: THE YORKSHIRE HOUSE PUBLIC HOUSE

This old public house stands in an area with a monastic history which stretches from the public house itself all the way down to the river where the Black Friars had their monastery since the thirteenth century.

The public house has the ghost of a woman and child who live upstairs and never cause a problem to anyone but it is the occasional visitor, a monk, which brings evil to the premises when he appears.

It was speaking to the licensee which gave me the confidence to mention my four-feet-tall creature which 'exuded evil' because he has experienced something similar. He was sleeping upstairs one Christmas guarding the extra stock which had been delivered for the holiday period. The licensee was awakened by noises just outside his bedroom door and was in no doubt that someone had broken in. He quietly stood on a chair and looked through the gap between the top of the door and the actual frame and in the corridor outside he saw a figure of a monk dressed in a cowl. His description made my blood run cold. *'It exuded absolute evil.'* And if you remember those were the only words I could find to describe my creature. The difference was that although my 'thing' was silent, his was babbling and whispering away to itself as it walked along the upstairs corridor before disappearing through the outside wall.

At least it is not just me who has experienced something I would not want to repeat.

ST MARY'S PLACE: THE OLD ROYAL SALOP INFIRMARY

The present building dates from the 1820s but stands just above the site of the Dominican Friars Priory, a hospital order of monks so there is a nice continuity of usage for the site. The Dominicans wore black habits so it should come as no surprise that one such monk prowls the corridors of the former hospital.

The old hospital was replaced in the 1970s by a new one in an out of town location and so the building is now the home to small specialist shops and, as well as our monk, the premises have more ghosts than any other single building in the town.

In what used to be an old operating theatre a Chinese restaurant once opened. Every night before going home the staff would clean up and set the tables for the following day. And every morning when they returned, all of the cutlery they'd set out was found to have been thrown onto the floor. As soon as they found out that it was the ghost of an old matron who was responsible they left. But you cannot blame the matron as all she was doing was to continue doing her job. She used to check the surgical instruments for cleanliness and any that she was unhappy with she threw onto the floor.

There is a Grey Lady in the old hospital which as you know, makes her the third Grey Lady of Shrewsbury. She is not to be confused with the one in the Lion Hotel or the one in the Wheatsheaf public house. This one used to appear at the foot of a patient's bed and was seen writing something.

This was not a good sign for the patient for she was writing out the death certificate. And her appearance as a harbinger of someone passing on was proved time and time again.

Where the toilets are today is where the hospital kitchens used to be. The kitchen staff were very kind to an old tramp and he has never left us. He shows his appreciation for the kindness he received by doing favours for the visitors to the kitchens today. He opens the doors to the toilet cubicles, but only for the ladies.

A nurse can be seen near to the staircase at the eastern end of the building and it is thought her dress is that from the time of the First World War. She is a shy person for as soon as you see her she promptly disappears. She is also to be found in the corner of the little shop tucked away at the bottom of those stairs only here you only ever get to see the bottom half of her.

In two other shops there have been some very peculiar 'goings-on.' Doors which are propped open by heavy weights will close of their own accord and wall displays of photographs etc. will be taken down overnight and carefully arranged in order around the room. They are placed directly beneath where they were hanging. As the units are individually locked as well as the outer doors being secured by modern locks, there can be no logical explanation as to what is happening.

However, if proof were needed I think we have some in this particular location. A researcher for a television company was in one of the gift shops asking about the ghosts for a programme that was to be made. As he was talking and being somewhat sceptical about the stories of doors closing on their own and what have you, a pack of paper napkins took itself off a wall mounted display, moved to the centre of the room and then was thrown onto his foot. At the same time the ceiling display above his head began to rotate rapidly.

During the course of one night tour I was taking and therefore only visiting the outside of the shop unit I have just referred to, a man took a photograph and was amazed to find that he had captured a single orb of light shooting upwards.

ST MARY'S PLACE: THE DRAPERS' HALL

The Drapers' Guild have owned their hall on the site since 1485. It is the oldest timber framed building in the country to have had uninterrupted sole occupancy. The present hall dates from 1576 and one of the dining rooms contains a fine fireplace with a date of 1658.

The dining room stands just inside the three ground floor windows and does have one resident ghost. The ethereal figure of a female form sometimes appears against the wall to be found on the other side of the window to the farthest left. She does nothing except keep the lucky diners company.

Drapers' Hall.

DOGPOLE

Leaving St Mary's Place and turning to the left we enter the ancient thoroughfare of Dogpole, a name taken from *'ducken'* meaning *'to stoop'* and *'pole'* meaning *'summit.'* It is likely that there was an inner wall to the town at the top of the Wyle Cop which had a small door in it sufficiently low to make the pedestrian bow his or her head to gain access to Dogpole.

THE OLD HOUSE

The Old House on Dogpole is a timber framed building dating from the early 1500s and once belonged to Anthony Rocke, a servant of Mary Tudor who was a daughter to Henry VIII by Katherine of Aragon. The house displays pomegranate adornments inside, the pomegranate being the badge of the ill fated Katherine. Mary Tudor used to stay in the house when, on behalf of her father, she attended the Council of the Marches during their sessions in Shrewsbury.

The house is heavily haunted. At the front door a ghost is often seen and described as *'glowing in the mist.'* In the cellar there is the smell of bacon frying and the sound of wood being chopped whilst on the staircase a child plays hide and seek. Everywhere there are whisperings and the sounds of footsteps.

There was one report of a noisy old man in the house but whether he is responsible for the 'whisperings,' the footsteps or the chopping of the wood, I do not know.

THE OLD CARRIAGE WORKS

Attached to the Old House is the recently renovated Old Carriage Works which now contains a number of apartments. One of these residences abuts the Old House and the new inhabitants of it have become a *'bit concerned.'* I'll let the owners do their own talking:

> *'Put it like this the presence in my bedroom is unsettling. It is enough to make a middle aged, unbelieving sceptic to get up out of bed in the middle of the night and leave the room.'*

NUMBER 12 DOGPOLE

12 Dogpole also enjoys the name London House. It is a merchant's house dating from the 1600s and is now a shop.

The staff there have certainly come across something 'strange' in the attic but it is the ghosts of an old man and his dog in the cellar which can be disconcerting. The small dog yaps away and the old man has taken a particular dislike to one girl who works there. When she is about things fly off the shelves as if they had been thrown at her.

The owner has one method of control over her guest. She has cleaned the cellar up and left a chair down there for the ghost to sit on. If he starts acting up in her presence it is a case of, *'Come on now. I have cleaned the place up. You have got a chair to sit on. Just think what it was like before I arrived here.'*

And that seems to calm him down at least for her – and for a while.

ST ALKMUND'S CHURCH

This church stands in the centre of Saxon Shrewsbury and was surrounded by the King's Market which outgrew the allotted space by the 1200s. The church itself was built between 912 and 920 A.D. by Ethelfreda of the Mercians who was the daughter of Alfred the Great and ruled the area in her own right after the death of her husband. She dedicated the church to St Alkmund *'from whom she was descended.'* His bones rested in the church before being sent to All Saints in Derby.

The church spire dates from medieval times and has a legend attached to it. It is that the devil himself climbs the

St Alkmund's Square.

tower so that he can look over toward the Stiperstones, a range of hills about twenty kilometres to the south to see if anyone is sitting on his 'Devil's Chair.' If he sees anyone is sitting on that rocky outcrop he calls down a great storm to show his displeasure. His claw marks are said to be at the top of the tower and are marks very like the amulet we spoke of earlier where you put your thumb between your forefinger and middle finger and say, *'Four fingers and a thumb witch, I defy thee.'*

If you look up you never know, you may just see the devil climbing the tower.

FISH STREET: THE THREE FISHES PUBLIC HOUSE

When you look up and see someone climbing the spire of St Alkmund's it may not be the devil. It could be George Arthur, a travelling steeplejack who used to drink in the Three Fishes when he was working in town.

Back in the 1400s George was having a drink in the public house and did what most steeplejacks did in those days to boost their income. He wagered that he could climb St Alkmund's right to the very top and spin the weathercock. He did it and won the wager which he spent on more rum. Then there was another bet that he couldn't do it again. George gave it a try, only being a little the worse for drink he fell and plummeted to his death in Fish Street.

George is still climbing the spire, so let us hope if you see the climber one dark night that it is George, not the devil.

Fish Street toward Butcher Row.

The Three Fishes has ghosts of its own inside the premises. Footsteps are heard upstairs when there cannot be anyone up there and the cellar is described as *'creepy'* and *'you are not alone.'*

But best of all is the young lady who comes from the kitchen with your food order. She is carrying the plates but if she enters the bar through the wall and not the door then you can be sure the meal is not yours.

FISH STREET: THE HAIRDRESSER'S SHOP

The house where John Wesley first preached Methodism in Shrewsbury in 1761 is now a hairdresser's shop. When they first opened for business curlers would be found near a bin on the floor and not in their proper place. It was as if the ghost had been amusing 'himself' by trying to throw one curler at a time into the basket.

I use the word 'himself' as when the niece of the owner came to stay in the accommodation above the shop she would spend the night talking to *a nice old man* who would sit at the foot of her bed.

This story is very familiar to me as my grandfather who brought me up in a pit village near Newcastle upon Tyne told me of a tale which happened to him when the family first arrived on Tyneside before the First World War. The family were poor and so he had to share his bed with a number of his brothers. Both he and 'Albie' spoke practically every night to *'an old man who sat at the foot of the bed.'*

In their case they discovered that the chap had been a schoolteacher before he had hanged himself in that very same bedroom. I wonder if something similar had occurred in Fish Street.

Fish Street toward St Julian's Chapel.

FISH STREET: THE ORREL

The Orrel is a building which forms part of a series of buildings collectively known as 'The Bear Steps.' They date from

the late 1500s to the early 1600s although there were buildings there certainly 200 years earlier.

The Orrel backs onto St Alkmund's churchyard and is a split-level building. I think that the building was cut into the burial ground and offer the next ghost as evidence for this. Appearing inside the Orrel and against the rearmost wall is the ghost of a man. He is tall and naked and has been split right down the middle from head to foot leaving him just half the width he should be. We know he is a kind man and that he was a Christian from the fact that he is surrounded by a blue light. From folk lore we know that a blue light associated with ghosts is good, that the person was a Christian and that no evil can take place in its immediate vicinity.

BUTCHER ROW: THE ABBOT'S HOUSE

Butcher Row is a medieval street once associated with the slaughter of animals brought there from the nearby King's Market. The beasts were slaughtered in the street and the jointed carcasses sold in the 41 butchers' shops which abounded nearby. The animal fat was rendered down for the candle makers and the skins sold to the tanners.

It is not surprising then that a number of premises in the short street have reported 'light orbs' in their premises.

However, in the Abbot's House which belonged to Shrewsbury Abbey and was part of their property portfolio to bring in money for their Order, there is a more easily identifiable ghost or ghosts. Although the Abbot never lived on the premises which date from the 1460s, it is also famous for its blue images appearing behind the ground floor windows. In the dead of night when you walk by there is certainly something which makes you feel as though a pair of eyes is watching you.

BUTCHER ROW: THE PRINCE RUPERT HOTEL

This hotel stands directly opposite the Abbot's House and is attached to a public house next door called 'The Bull.' It was surprising to me that the Bull had no ghosts. As the licensee said, *'The only spirits we have got are behind the bar in bottles.'* But just as I thought 'ah, well, you can't win them all,' someone else present mentioned the kitchen cutlery tray which had been thrown to the floor or the glasses which have rolled off the bar. The bar staff denied all knowledge of these events but they are explained and rationalised away.

But you can't rationalize away the man in the trilby, 'a solid shadow,' walking through the adjoining wall of the Prince Rupert before going upstairs and disappearing along the first floor corridor.

The Bull public house is attached to the hotel which takes its name from Prince Rupert, the right hand man of Charles I during the Civil War. Rupert was in charge of the garrison of royalist troops stationed in Shrewsbury during that period and requisitioned the property from its owner, 'Jones the Rich' who had just spent a fortune renovating the place.

The building stands on cellars and foundations that are at least one thousand years old and it is in these cellars that we find some unpleasantness. Although the underlying reasons

An orb in the cellar of the Prince Rupert.

are still unknown it is possible that the ghosts have something to do with a skeleton which was once found under the floor of the cellar.

There is certainly an angry man down there, a shadowy figure in the corner and he is accompanied by a cold draught. Bearing in mind that this cellar was in total darkness, the opportune click of a camera has given us the picture of an energy orb just at the place the angry man inhabits. Is it his spirit?

Room 7 of the hotel is reputed to be haunted, some saying by the ghost of a bride who hanged herself in there. Another would have it that it is a bridegroom looking for the girl who jilted him. I don't know, but the second version sits very nicely with the ghost of a general in the royalist army, an aide to Prince Rupert who was also staying in the headquarters building.

The night before he was to marry a local girl, she ran off with a lieutenant. Presumably he was a lot younger than the general. The older man still walks the corridors outside the bedrooms opening the doors as he goes to look for his lost bride – or to get even with the lieutenant.

In 1984 the film *Christmas Carol* was shot in Shrewsbury by our friends from Hollywood. It was the version with George C. Scott taking the lead role of Scrooge. The film crew set up their headquarters in the hotel and one evening one of the producers was on his way to bed when he saw an elderly man coming toward him along the narrow passageway. The chap was wearing a nightshirt and one of those night caps which hangs down to one side of the head. He was also carrying a candle.

It struck our Californian cousin that this was somewhat strange but put it down to the eccentricity for which the English are famed. The man made no reply to the American's, *"Good night,"* and it was only then that realisation dawned on him. The candle cast no light so he turned – just in time to see the apparition walk through a closed door.

The producer spent the rest of the night in the bar.

A CONCLUSION

I do hope you have enjoyed this adventure into the darker side of Saxon Scrobbs-by-rig, today's Shrewsbury. We have met some of the 600 or so ghosts who reputedly inhabit our town along with today's population. Some of the ghosts have been 'verified' by psychic researchers, others by being seen by more than one person on different occasions. Do we have photographic 'evidence' of yet more?

I know what experiences I have had and I guess that is as good a place as any to bring this to an end. All I can do is let you in on what I know or have learned and then you make your own mind up.

By the way, one last thought as you prepare to leave Shrewsbury. The good news is that witches will not follow you across water, so exit by the English or Welsh Bridges. And just to be doubly sure, do what folklore from the Scottish Borders tells you to do. Spit three times into the water below to ensure a safe passage.

Well – you can never be too careful, just in case.

GOD BLESS